I'M GETTING
THOSE COOKIES
An Incredible Way To Capture
What You See Everyday

Dr. J. Edward Dukes

I'm Getting Those Cookies
An Incredible Way to Capture What You See Everyday

Copyright © 2016 by Dr. J. Edward Dukes

ISBN: 978-0-692-78880-6

Printed in the Unites States of America

Published by BRJ Ministries, Inc.

TABLE OF CONTENTS

DEDICATION

This book is dedicated to Al,
who asked me that question in the basement
and the fellowship that helped me answer it.

REVIEW

I'm Getting Those Cookies is a must read for anyone who has stood on the sidelines cheering and providing support for the dreams of others knowing there is more. I LOVE THIS BOOK! I laughed, I cried, it made me think, it stirred me. *I'm Getting Those Cookies* provides practical advice and steps in activating your own dreams one decision at a time. It is an OUTSTANDING and very well written book to unlock your destiny. I highly recommend this book!! THIS BOOK IS HUGE!!

Beverly Moore

FOREWORD

This is my father's labor of love. A process that started as a young fatherless boy with dreams and tears has emerged into a great work of encouragement and inspiration.

I know first hand the power of your words, your illustrations, and your directions. I am confident that this book, your words, will do for others what you have done for me.

Thank you for protecting me from dangers seen and unseen. Thank you for making sure I never became "that chick." Thank you for teaching me how to ride my bike and drive a car.

Thank you for being there after my first accident and my second. Thank you for helping me get over my first heartbreak. Thank you for coming to all my poetry slams and telling me I was better than everyone even though I knew those kids had bars.

Thank you for taking me on my first date, my first vacation, sending me my first love letter (from Africa), for all the meet and greets, all the balls and galas, and all the opportunities. Thank you for cursing me out, taking all my clothes and my right shoes to humble me.

Thank you for teaching me "men are hunters," "never be too available," and "don't come out asshole backwards." Just thank you, Daddy, because I never would be the woman I am without you being the man you are. A girl's standards and values are set by her father and thank you for setting mine so high. I've seen you, a fatherless child, be a father not only to my brothers, and my cousins but me as well. I don't mind sharing my Daddy with the world because he has so much to share. I love you, Daddy!

I am going to get those cookies.

Emerald Valere Dukes
"The Tallest Tree In The Forest"

INTRODUCTION

Capacity |kə'pasitē|
The maximum amount that something can contain

Capability |kāpə'bilitē|
The extent of someone's or something's ability

Competency |kämpətənsē|
The ability to do something successfully or efficiently

Each day we come face to face with ideas, ambitions, and dreams that we harbor within us but yet never bring them to fruition. We watch as others fulfill our dreams, birth our ideas and live lives of fulfillment and accomplishment. When we see others doing what we know we can do, when we see others living how we know we should be living and when we see others being who we know we should be, a serious question is raised: What about me? The daily reminders that we see every day that seems so distant and out of reach can become our motivation and inspiration. Whatever journey brought you to this very sentence is all part of the centricity of your success. The fact that this book is in your hands at this precise moment reflects the true nature of its writings: the things that have eluded you are actually in your grasp.

What in particular is in your grasp? A very slippery concept called, realizing your potential. That's it! I said it on the first page but let's actualize your potential.

The problem we all face is identifying our potential. So often we hear others say we have so much potential. We graciously say thank you and leave questioning our potential: to do what, to become what, or to see what they see. By the time we realize the possibilities of our potential, many of us believe it's too late in our lives or careers to ever become what so many people saw previously. This is the moment when you become a spectator in life and watch others become, prosper, achieve success, and make their dreams come true.

I have good news-it is not too late for you! To be honest, now is the best time for you to tap into that reservoir of potential that has been lying dormant in your life for so many years. I really wish that our potential was voice activated and we could just speak to that potential within us; that it would come to life and magically begin to work towards our dreams.

Unfortunately, it is not. Hard work is a prerequisite for success and the realization of dreams. In addition, we must accept and confront some truths and some misconceptions about ourselves so that we can transform from dream state to reality being.

There are three key components that are essential if we are going to be victorious at transitioning from dream state to reality being, from potential to greatness, and from spectator to participator. These three components that need extensive attention are your capacity, capability, and competency. The development or enlarging of your capacity, capability and competency will enhance your possibilities of success, self-actualization, and getting what you see every day.

This book is my effort to help develop and enlarge your capacity (the amount that you can contain), capability (your ability to perform), and competency (the ability to do what you perform successfully and efficiently). The question becomes, how do you do it? You must become deliberate in your efforts to reduce the distance between what you see every day and where you are right now. This is the mission that we will take on together - reducing the distance. We must embrace the idea that dreams still come true, miracles are real, and we have greatness within us. We will close the gap and make the unreachable reachable and the impossible possible.

CHAPTER 1
Auntie's Cookie Jar

"First they ignore you, then they laugh at you, then they fight you, then you win."
~ Gandhi

I have many fond memories as a child. My life was filled with typical boyhood adventures and dreams. I would embark on journeys in my mind of being the greatest football player, being an astronaut and soaring over the world, or maybe going back in time and changing history. I had an assortment of boy dolls, aka action figures (the term of the day) that I would use to reenact scenes from my favorite movies, cartoons and the vast amount of books that I read. I would envision being the Six Million Dollar Man, Incredible Hulk, Spiderman, Huck Finn or being in the land of the Wizard of Oz.

I loved having unlimited possibilities, untapped potential, and a vivid imagination. It gave me the ability to transcend what was around me and become whoever I wished to be.

A critical part of my childhood was my dear mother's impartation. As a single mother of five, she exposed me to a wealth of intellectual and spiritual information that has been a tremendous help in navigating through my adult life. Mother and I would talk about the rich history of her Mississippi upbringing, the Great Migration North and how she as a teenage girl boarded a train to Chicago to live a life of dreams in the big city. Mother taught me the importance of spiritual maintenance and the power of prayer. I remember learning how to pray and reciting the familiar childhood bedtime prayer:

Now I lay me down to sleep,
I pray the Lord my soul to keep.
If I should die before I wake,
I pray to God my soul to take.

That prayer was kind of morbid and a little scary for a child. As I think about it, I'm glad I made it through the night.

The majority of these wisdom conversations with my mother would occur on Saturday mornings. I have distinct memories of Saturday mornings in particular. I would awake to the sound of my mother praying and making coffee; which was her daily routine. I would grab my favorite box of cereal, plop in front of the television and watch Saturday morning cartoons. For those who can relate, you remember those Saturday morning cartoons: Schoolhouse Rock with Conjunction Junction, I'm Just A Bill and Three Is A Magic Number. What about Hong Kong Phooey, Scooby Doo, Super Friends and of course Tom and Jerry? As I enjoyed my countless bowls of cereal and all my favorite cartoons, I would eagerly await the moment that I could join my mother on her Saturday errands. One errand in particular I enjoyed was grocery shopping. I loved grocery shopping with my mother. Grocery shopping was a monthly adventure, and it was a major event in our household. I can still hear my siblings asking, "Mama, when you going grocery shopping?" "Mama don't forget to get this, Mama we need this or we just ran out of that." While I was watching cartoons and eating cereal, mother would be busy making the grocery list. Once she completed the grocery list, we were in the car and on our way to our Saturday adventure, which included a stop at the local grocery store.

Mother and I had a system, she would place me in the cart, then hand me the grocery list. As we went from aisle to aisle, I would call out what was on the grocery list. Mother would retrieve the items and pass them to me. I would place them in the basket and scratch that item off the list. I was her official little helper.

My favorite section in the entire grocery store was the cookie aisle. As we turned the corner to enter the aisle, I was greeted with what seemed like a million varieties of cookies. The selection was extensive and varied in taste and texture: oatmeal, oatmeal and raisin, butter, peanut butter, fig, sandwich cookies, frosty lemon, black and white, English biscuits, Christmas, fortune, almond, gingerbread, shortbread, macaroon, sugar, windmill, fudge stripe, wafer, and, my favorite, chocolate chip. Every month I got the opportunity to pick out the cookies. I was the man because I was in charge of the cookie selection. That was a major job for a six-year-old with four siblings. I couldn't wait to get home and show my siblings what cookies I had picked. I was the official cookie picker, and I wore that title with pride. I was always on the hunt for the best cookie in the world.

As my mother and I were returning from Saturday morning grocery shopping, we visited my aunt's house. I was excited when my mother made the unannounced stop. I loved my aunt's house because she always had special treats for me. It was here that I saw something I had never seen before in my entire six years of living.

I proceeded across the well-manicured lawn into the side door that led directly into the kitchen. As an inquisitive youth, I surveyed my auntie's kitchen; I was in search of those treats that made my auntie famous in my eyesight. Maybe I would spot a bowl of candy, a taffy apple, a fresh baked pie or cake, some chips or popcorn, or a juicy piece of fruit.

As I scanned the high countertops, to my amazement and delight, I saw the most beautiful chocolate chips cookies in the whole wide world. They were magnificent in color, giant in size and moist in appearance. The chips were so enormous that they appeared to be bursting out of every part of the cookie. They were as thick as my hand and perfectly round. There was something very different about these cookies. It was not their impeccable appearance, flawless shape, their gigantic size nor their lovely color, but it was the container. These beautiful cookies were in a glass jar with a lid on a counter that was well out of my reach; in something my auntie called a cookie jar. This bothered me because those wonderful cookies seemed trapped, confined and inaccessible. I was not accustomed to seeing cookies on display. The cookies at our house, in our kitchen, were tucked away in the cabinet or eaten at once.

I asked my auntie with a great amount of expectation and enthusiasm, "Can I have one of those marvelous cookies?" and she said, "No... not right now, it's still morning". Why would anyone show you cookies, lock them up, put them out of reach and tell you NO? That is cruel and unusual punishment. Why show them to me and tell me NO? Why put them out if you are not going to give them out? Why let me see them if I can't have one? I had many questions and no answers. But one thing I did know, I was ***getting those cookies***.

CHAPTER 2
Think Big, Live Large and Dream Enormous

"When I was a child, I spoke as a child,
I understood as a child, I thought as a
child; but when I became a man,
I put away childish things."
~ Apostle Paul

In the context of this book, a cookie is a metaphor for our dreams, aspirations, and ambitions. And, the cookie jar represents everything that we must go through to get what we desire. As an adult, we don't spend our days and hours trying to devise strategies to get freshly baked cookies, but we do need to identify what type of cookies rests within the cookie jar, and what we need to do to access it.

As I grew from child to adult, I had awe-inspiring dreams, created lofty aspirations, and have been filled with unyielding ambition. My mantra is think big, live large and dream enormous. Our dreams, aspirations, and ambitions are not to be sealed in a glass jar for observation purposes only; they are to be enjoyed like those cookies at my auntie's house with a tall cold glass of milk or a big bowl of ice cream.

My auntie's cookies were just the first of many challenges that I had to conquer in life. Childhood cookies should evolve into adult cookies so that dreams, aspirations and ambitions will be realized and not remain a fantasy.

Life has the peculiar ability to show you what it has to offer and at the same time deny you participation. Reminders of what we don't have and what we really desire through television, advertising, magazines, and movies constantly surround us. You can wish all you want about the things life shows you. You can read about them in magazines or see them on television, but the truth of the matter is we are just looking at cookies in a jar. Adult cookies represent the collective experiences of life. I can see the cookies I want, but the cookie jar is out of reach, and I don't have permission to open the lid to enjoy what lies within.

As adults, our cookie jar holds cookies like joy, happiness, rewards, pleasures, achievements, and promotions; which have a direct connection to our dreams. Just as the cookie jar on my auntie's counter needed to be opened, so too does the cookie jar of your life. The adult cookie represents a multitude of things that we believe we could have, things we may even deserve, but always seem to be out of reach. We need to be able to reach in and get those things we have exposure to but have no access, the metaphoric cookie.

Examples of cookies that adults often seek:

- The successful business cookie: a business that has satisfied customers, that yield profits, employs dedicated talented people and will establish generational wealth for the owner.

- The enriching career cookie: one that my skills are optimized, earn an excellent salary, awesome benefits, and are in a positive and productive work environment.

- The love cookie: the ability to give and receive love unconditionally. To have trusting relationships/companionships that have support, encouragement, and understanding.

- The happy family cookie: the ability to have minimal household drama, spend quality time together, truly uplift each other and happy to be around one another.

- The life-changing cookie: the ability to be connected and involved with making a difference in people's lives through community, ministry, volunteering or mentoring.

- The world travel cookie: simply wanting to see the world through the multiplicity of cultures, foods, people and places.

- The financial freedom cookie: being able to accumulate wealth, be debt free and have the capacity to do what you want without the restriction of money.

- The peace of mind cookie: being able to find harmony, joy, and oneness with yourself and community.

- The dream cookie: being able to believe and have faith in the impossible no matter how farfetched.

GET THOSE COOKIES

As we grow and mature, these are the types and varieties of cookies that are in our cookie jar as adults. We must maintain a positive perspective and attitude of achievement to get the cookies that we see others enjoy daily. I can say with a great amount of confidence and conviction, we **want those cookies**.

CHAPTER 3
A Matter of Taste

"The courage to be is the courage to accept oneself, in spite of being unacceptable."
~ Paul Tillich

As a child, I recall many things that I was prohibited from eating or drinking. My consumption of such things as shrimp, crab legs, gumbo, steak or beverages like beer, alcohol, and Pepsi were considered for adults only. As a matter of fact, I was told I would not enjoy their taste because it was an "acquired taste." I had no idea what an "acquired taste" was, but I did know you had to be an adult to have one.

As I grew older and my experiences expanded, travel and exposure to different cultures broadened. I began to acquire a taste for things I never had while growing up in Chicago. I was acquiring a taste for new and different things. When you acquire a taste for something, it means you've learned to ignore the perceived negative qualities in order to enjoy its benefits. We learn to bypass its weird look, it's funny smell or the simple fact we never had it before. Or you learn to like something because that is all that is available to you. My friend told me he grew up on a farm and he remembers seeing tomatoes everywhere he looked. His family ate every sort of tomato dish imaginable. I asked him so you just love tomatoes and he responded, "Absolutely not, I hate them." He only ate tomatoes because that was the only thing available. Your taste for many things can be based on a variety of circumstances, necessities, indulgences or privileges.

What's amazing is that as we get older, we are exposed to and experience these different tastes. People differ in their preferences. Some people love the taste of sweet and seek things that satisfy that craving. Others may have an appetite for sour, bitter or salty things. Consumption and the exposure to these different tastes happen gradually. Nearly all humans graduate from a childhood love of sweet to more complex flavors as adults. Exposure and experiences have created a new taste; one that is far different than when we were young and limited. This graduation can be attributed to taking a risk, trying new things, experiencing a different culture or simply acquiring a penchant for something unusual.

As we move into adulthood, we should become more expansive and complex with our appetite, no longer seeking the simple satisfaction from the chocolate chip cookies in the cookie jar. As an adult, the question becomes, what has become our preference and our acquired taste? What is our particular choice? Has our appetite evolved, or are we still enjoying the same old cookies?

What life experiences altered your appetite, your taste buds if you will (your choices, your dreams, your goals, and ambitions)? At some point in your growing up and experiencing life on life's terms, those taste buds were modified. It is safe to say that your taste has adjusted over time.

We have long known that the fundamental tastes are sweet, sour, bitter and salty. If we were to categorize our life experiences into sweet, sour, bitter and salty, it would become obvious that we have acquired some different preferences and new tastes.

This means that as adults we have encountered some sweet times, endured our share of sour moments, have a few bitter regrets and withstood salty relationships. These collective encounters create a heightened sensitivity to what we like and don't like, shaped our view of the world as adults and made us make some significant adjustments to our childhood craving for sweets only. Our lives have expanded, our appetites have grown, and our interaction with others have influenced our choices and decisions.

We must pause to reflect and evaluate how these sweet, sour, bitter and salty moments have truly affected our perspective of the world and ourselves.

- The sweet times: graduations, weddings, first house, new car, babies, perfect job, promotions, or entrepreneurship.

- The sour moments: dropping out, major mistakes in judgment, incarceration, addiction, bankruptcy, foreclosure, death of loved ones, or getting cut from the team.

- The bitter regrets: school choice, moving too soon, staying too late, marriage, divorce, abortions, having children, or quitting.

- The salty relationships: parents, spouses, children, coworkers, bosses, friends and lovers.

Ask yourself, what was my preference before and after those sweet, sour, bitter and salty encounters? Did my taste change because of my experiences, exposures or my maturity? Did I acquire a taste for something for that particular moment or do I still hunger for the cookies of yesterday? What cookies am I really seeking, the cookies of my past, the cookies of my present or the cookies of my future? These are all questions that you should ask yourself at this point.

Our first desire, before we became adults, was for anything sweet. As a matter of fact, scientific evidence proves that a child's first acknowledgment of taste is sweetness. Guess what, we have never lost that as our primary indicator of what we consider to be good.

When you were a child you walked around saying, "When I grow up, I want to be this..." and, "When I grow up, I want to have that." "I want a car like that, a house like that." You had dreams that didn't even match your talent or your skill set, but it didn't stop you from dreaming it. The truth is you never stop wanting what is sweet in life. In some instances, you've allowed your experiences and exposures to cause you to lose your ambition. You adjusted your taste, curbed your appetite, and as a result, you've become average, but your dreams are still in that cookie jar.

What happened to your passion, your drive, and your get-up-and-go-get-it attitude? When did you decide that everything had to come to you, and when did you become satisfied watching others enjoy their cookies?

You are not a spectator, you are a participator. Just think about all of life's challenges you have already overcome. The obstacles you have already faced and conquered. And now you want to stop without your cookies? No way! You deserve those cookies! You deserve to enjoy them!

Can you remember the sweet smell of fresh baked cookies? You couldn't wait to get a big glass of milk or a bowl of ice cream to go with them. Do you remember how wonderful those warm gooey cookies that just melt in your mouth were? Never forget that taste of satisfaction. Because that is how sweet and wonderful your dreams, aspirations, and ambitions will taste and smell. Never forget the joy that overtook you when you knew exactly the pleasure that you were about to experience from indulging in the warm gooey cookies.

GET THOSE COOKIES

Today you must identify what cookies you like and set your mind on how you will get the things you see and desire every day that appears to be out of reach. Today is that someday you have been waiting on and talking about. I know you have had this conversation with yourself: "Well someday things are going to turn around for me, someday I am going to start my own, someday I am going to start again, and someday it's going to be my turn." Well, guess what? Today is that day; not Monday, Tuesday, Wednesday, Thursday, Friday, Saturday or Sunday. Today is that someday.

And this is the day *you're **getting those cookies!!!***

CHAPTER 4
Access Denied

Those who say it can't be done are
usually interrupted by others doing it
~ James A. Baldwin

It is a Father's Day tradition that my family and I gather for a weekend of just plain fun and excitement. I thoroughly enjoy spending quality family time just laughing and being adventurous. It is my personal subscription to keeping young, connected and loved. We have in the past frequented such places as: theme parks, camping grounds, and water sports outings.

Recently, my family and I visited Wisconsin Dells, the self-proclaimed, "Water park capital of the world." We did our due diligence and searched the Internet for the best deal with the most fun. We wanted to get the most bang for our buck. We were in search of convenience, comfort, economical cost and somewhere suitable for all ages to accommodate our family. We found an online advertisement that read:

For the surprisingly low price of $35 per person /per day, you can enjoy a 70-acre family water park with both thrill and child-friendly slides, lazy rivers, wave pools and more. You'll know right away you're somewhere special. Featuring an exciting mix of excitement, from our amazing water park to our thrilling Indoor Theme Park, we offer an array of attractions for children of all ages, whether they're 3, 13 or 30 and up.

This description fits our desires. We jumped in the car and headed to the resort to enjoy all the amenities that were offered for the incredible price of $35 per person/per day. We paid the fee and entered with great anticipation and excitement seeking the rides and thrills that were promised. Quickly, my daughter began to realize that we could not enter and enjoy *every* ride. She would try to gain access and would be denied because her wristband did not give her complete access to everything the water park had to offer. We were in the facility, we could see the rides, we could even see others enjoying the thrills, but we were limited due to access. As it turns out, there was one fee for entrance into the park and yet another fee for full access.

This is indicative of many things in life, once you have been accepted, you realize you don't have complete access; you are limited. It takes something extra to gain full access. That something extra will always cost you something. You have to pay a price to get what you initially thought you would receive when you committed

We will do or pay anything to gain access because it was initially denied. We have houses, garages, attics, basements, desks and computers full of stuff we just had to have; not because it was necessary, but because we had to have access. Just imagine if you would take that same thought process and apply that energy to something that matters. Apply that ingenuity in areas in your life that will yield a return on your efforts. Apply that creativity to areas in your life where you are good, but if you fully committed, you would become great. Talented people can always do average things because they have talent. But at some point average is not good enough. You want more and if you want more, you must lock into that one thing and work it with everything you've got to gain access, not just exposure. I know with certainty you want to do more than just enter the park and see the rides, you want to ride all the rides.

Therefore, you must work on things that matter and things that will make a measurable positive change in your life. Things that should matter to you are: recapturing lost dreams and forgotten passions, establishing a strong family foundation, and aligning yourself with your purpose.

As we go through our daily lives, we quickly learn that many closed cookie jars surround us in our lives. There are many rides we just can't enjoy. We make attempts to gain access but are consistently denied. Our lives are filled with extra cost, restrictions, requirements, and flat out "no's"; basically, cookies that we see but cannot enjoy. We see those opportunities just as I saw those cookies in my Auntie's cookie jar; visible, but not attainable.

GET THOSE COOKIES

Are you going to get this close, where you can see it and hear others enjoy it? I know you're not going to just walk away disappointed. You should care less about the extra cost, restrictions, requirements, and "no's." Do you see what you want? Is it in front of you? Then get prepared to take that lid off the cookie jar and *GET THOSE COOKIES*.

CHAPTER 5
Guess What? Me, Too.

*"I hated every minute of training, but I
said, 'Don't quit. Suffer now and live
the rest of your life as a champion.'"*
~ Muhammad Ali

Okay, let's start where most people quit. Most people quit when obstacles and challenges arise and in turn, they make excuses for why they can't keep going.

Obstacles: barriers, hurdles, stumbling blocks, obstructions, impediments, hindrances, snags, catches, drawbacks, hitches, handicaps, deterrents, complications, difficulties, problems, disadvantages, curves, restraints, restrictions, limitations, encumbrances, interferences, delays, setbacks, inconveniences, nuisances, disadvantages...

Challenges: tests, questionings, disputes, stand-offs, oppositions, confrontations, problems, difficult tasks, trials.

Excuses: justify, defend, condone, vindicate; forgive, overlook, disregard, ignore, tolerate, sanction, accept, allow, let pass, turn a blind eye, forget; pardon, let go.

To be more specific here is a list of typical excuses that aid in creating obstacles and challenges. These excuses over time become our reality and manifests in our minds as real obstacles and challenges. Not only do we tell ourselves these things, but ultimately we believe them.

- *This is as good as it gets; If it were for me, I would have had it by now*
- *Obviously, I don't have what it takes; It's my parent's fault*
- *If I didn't have kids; I married the wrong person*
- *If that didn't happen to me, I would have...*
- *I'm way too busy; something is better than nothing*
- *This is a young person's game; I missed my chance*

- *I'm way too old now; I'm too young*
- *I should have done that a long time ago; I should have never left*
- *I should have gone; I should have stayed*
- *I don't know where to start; I can't afford it right now*
- *I have too much to lose; I'm going to look stupid*
- *I will be the only one trying to do it; maybe next time*
- *I'm going to start tomorrow, or next week, or next month, or next year*
- *No one else has ever done this; I can't do it*
- *I can't get any help; I'm all by myself*
- *Nobody likes me; everybody is against me*

At the end of the day, your cookies are still in that jar, and you still can't taste them. Instead of being filled with cookies you are filled with excuses. Instead of having cookies in your hands, you have a fistful of challenges. You allow obstacles to blind and prevent you from success.

I have many instances in my life that can qualify as an obstacle, challenge or excuse. One, in particular, happened while I was in college. While in college, I experienced one of the most horrible moments of my life. I was in love, for real-for real. I was nineteen years old, attending school in Mississippi and the love of my life was at school in Southern Illinois. Distant lovers to say the least. We vowed to write and speak daily. Now these were the days before cell phones; believe it or not, people actually wrote letters. I purchased some very sophisticated stationery and sprayed my best cologne, "Grey Flannel," for the perfect intimate touch. I addressed each letter "Dear Peaches" and signed it "Love Boo Boo." She was Peaches, and I was proud to be Boo Boo. While on spring break I paid her a surprise visit, and boy was I surprised. Peaches had a new boyfriend. I was devastated and heartbroken.

We all have a "Peaches and Boo Boo" story; a moment in our lives where we never thought we would bounce back. We have all been lonely, misunderstood, overlooked, quit too soon, stayed too long, loved too hard, and trusted too much. And, yes, it hurts. It's devastating; emotionally, mentally and spirituality draining. You feel like giving up; and yes, you even feel like you are going to die, but yet you survived.

You sought a way to rise above whatever tried to take you away from your dreams, ambitions, and desires. And that is the very reason why you are reading this book today — to rise above.

Now you must devise a plan of action, create a strategy, think past your obstacles, confront your challenges and work through your excuses. This step is simple but not easy. By dealing with obstacles, challenges and excuses we reconnect with that latent potential, lost dreams awaken and new possibilities arise. This is how we will build and enlarge capacity, capability, and competency.

GET THOSE COOKIES

As I stood there looking up at those cookies, I knew were several things that stood between those beautiful, moist and tantalizing cookies and me. There were obstacles, challenges and a few valid excuses that prohibited me from getting what my eyes saw and my heart desired. First, I didn't have the capacity, I was too short. Second, I didn't have the capability, the skill set or the ingenuity to get to the cookies. Third, I didn't have the competency; I just didn't know enough to make a concentrated effort to get to the cookies. Lastly, I needed permission. In spite of all my justifiable obstacles, and convincing challenges, and valid excuses, none of them deterred me from wanting what I saw but could not reach. I still had to figure out a way to GET THOSE COOKIES!

CHAPTER 6
Winners Win And Losers Lose

The first man gets the oyster;
the second man gets the shell.
~ Andrew Carnegie

Some things in life do not require a lot of explanation. This chapter is one of those things.

I recently came to a defining moment in my life. It was a moment when all of a sudden everything seemed clear and less complicated. In professional sports, they refer to this as the game slowing down. Repetition, practice, coaching and competition all play an integral role in finally understanding what you are doing, why you are doing it and what the end result will be from you doing it.

I pursued a childhood dream of becoming an elected official. It has always been a desire of mine to run for office, to gain political power, and set in motion a dynasty of politicians like the Kennedy clan.

This was one of my cookies to be like the Kennedy clan. In my plan, I would be Joseph Kennedy, the patriarch of the family, the person who would establish my family's foundation as a political force. After vast amounts of prayer, meditation, and consultation, I made the decision to seek office. It was my time to go after my cookie.

What should be noted is that I am a pastor, motivational speaker, business owner, community activist, father, husband, and mentor. My plan for the election was to kick into high gear for office five months prior to the election. I believed I could work vigorously on my campaign for a solid five months and secure a victory. After all, I am charismatic, educated, influential, well informed and articulate in vast categories and social concerns. All I had to do is jump in the race at the last minute and win; it was that simple, so I thought. The problem was that my opponent, the victor, started running ten years prior. I, in contrast, the charismatic, educated, influential, well informed and articulate in vast categories and social concerns guy began five months prior. I lost. I lost not solely on the fact that I started late; I lost because I never had a plan to win. I saw what I wanted, and I said let's go get it. I never took into consideration the amount of time and energy needed to win. I did not gauge whether I had the capacity, capability, and competency to WIN. I absolutely had the capacity, capability, and competency to become a great elected official. But in order to be great, I had to first win.

I had a plan to start, but I didn't have a plan to win. In my mind starting and winning were synonymous; however, if you look in any thesaurus, you'll discover they are not the same. You have to have a vision of yourself with those cookies in your hand. Get rid of that defeatist mentality and old adages: at least I gave it the old college try, good things come to those that wait, or don't count your chickens before they hatch. Trying only means something to people that have grown accustomed to losing or waiting. I never run a race to come in second place because even in second place you are still a loser.

GET THOSE COOKIES

For you to get those cookies, it is going to require at least one win. Win baby win has to be your mindset; not what comes after the win but how do I position myself to get those cookies. The time of you living vicariously through someone else is over, that mentality is for losers. Those cookies you see, they are yours. I wrote this book so you can get those cookies, not try and get them, but actually have them in your hands and enjoy them. That is your primary focus, to do whatever it takes to increase your capacities, capabilities, and competencies to win. Anything else is unacceptable, period!

CHAPTER 7
It's Time To Get Personal

"Instructions for successful living:
Dream it. Plan it. Do it. Repeat it."
~ Steve Maraboli

In order for you to win, actualize dreams or just become better, it must be a personal quest. You must possess unyielding focus, passion and determination to become someone better or get something greater. That inner fire is crucial to staying the course to your expected end. I have a strong belief that you have that fire. My concern is, do you have a path to your cookies and will you follow it? The path to your cookies must be personal. The path cannot be borrowed, bought or stolen from anyone else. It must be birthed from within in order for it to work. It has to be so personal that it literally pains you every time you see the cookies but can't reach them. It should be so personal that it disturbs your sleep and interrupts your thoughts. It should make you angry when you cannot enjoy the cookies you see every day.

Remember, what I stated as I closed the introduction, this book is my effort to help develop and enlarge your capacity (the amount that you can contain), your capability (your ability to perform), and your competency (the ability to do what you perform successfully and efficiently). Each one creates personal development and enrichment; not the things around you but the things within you. You must take it personal!

The key question of this chapter is, how do we get you there? How do we transition from an entry level position to management, from the sidelines to being on the field, from last to first, from employee to employer, from good, to better, to best? The answer is hard work. This seems simple, and quite frankly it is that simple. The hard part is that it requires thinking. Thinking is where most people fall short. Many do not take the time or put thought into actually achieving or getting what they want and desire. It's a fleeting idea that brings temporary excitement with no action. Remember when we were children, and we would walk down the street saying, "When I grow up, I want a car or a house like that." We never thought how much work we would have to do to get that car or that house.

So, let's think about what's needed to be successful. It's imperative at this juncture that you grab a pen and write down these things that are a MUST for you to develop or enlarge your capacity, capability, and competency. In other words, you need a plan on how to get your cookies. Please don't make the same mistake I made in my pursuit of being an elected official. You cannot just wake up one day and say, "Hey that's what I always wanted" and expect to get it. Trust me, it doesn't work like that. You must create a path to success. If you don't, you are walking into a collision with failure. Your path must be comprehensive and strategic with the ability to yield positive outcomes and expected results. Each step you take will get you closer to those cookies.

Now let's get started and focus our attention on your "personal" path to those cookies.

VISION *(The Dream)*

Before you even think about taking the first step, you must first know where you are going. The 'Where you are going statement' is where you want to end, not where you want to be next. Those are two separate things. I want you to take the time and think about where you want to end, and that place is called your vision. Envision where you will be, envision those cookies in your hand.

Very simply, your vision is your dream. This is not the vision of a company, a church or a block club; this is your personal vision. Remember it must be personal. In Chapter 2 we discussed a few cookies adults seek. We even defined a few. Now it's time to take a closer look at those cookies and determine which one you are going to get. Shall it be the successful business cookie, the enriching career cookie, the love cookie, the happy family cookie, the life-changing cookie, the world travel cookie, the financial freedom cookie, the peace of mind cookie or the biggie, the dream cookie? Once you have made that decision, make your vision into a personal statement that is inspiring, understood, easy to communicate, and short enough to fit on a T-shirt.

For the purpose of illustration let's choose the life-changing cookie. The life-changing cookie is being able to be connected to a cause. It involves helping others and making a difference in people's lives through community, ministry, volunteering or mentoring.

It has always been a dream of mine to mentor a group of inner city fatherless boys and help navigate them to successful careers. I want to become involved in their lives as early as possible and help build esteem, character, and purpose. I want to help change the perceived trajectory of their lives, from gangs, school dropout, drugs, jail, or possibly death to productive members of society. I want to be instrumental in changing their lives. And, it is personal to me because I grew up without a father. I dreamed and imagined what it would be like to have a father that was present in my life. There were critical moments in my life where I needed guidance, direction, and love from a man. I embraced the absence of a man in my life; I used that absence as a catalyst to excel. And when I became an adult and a father, I developed a desire to help fill the void in fatherless boys.

This is my passion, my desire, and my life-changing cookie, to be with them from the cradle to a successful career. My personal vision statement for this illustration is "From Cradles to Careers." This personal vision statement defines my purpose, announces my intentions, establishes my starting point and clearly defines my end. And what is really awesome is that I can fit it on a T-shirt.

There you have it, my personal vision statement: "From Cradles to Careers."

Now it's time to write your personal vision statement based on your dreams, your passion, your adult cookies and what you see every day but can't seem to grasp. I promise you this seemingly minimal task is going to inspire, direct, and ignite your journey.

MISSION (The What and Why)

The first step on your path to get those cookies is to

to form a mission. Now that you have created a vision statement and know your final destination, you can begin to take some steps along the path to the cookies. You must have a mission and be on a mission. Whatever you do, please do not create an impossible mission. It needs to be simple. It needs to be attainable. It needs to satisfy your desires. This is crucial, you should only have one mission. You cannot go to multiple places at the same time. Once you have decided what your mission will be, be on a mission to accomplish it. Hint: If you cannot determine where the mission will take you, then you will arrive at a destination called "nowhere." The mission is supposed to create continuous and purposeful movement.

Your vision statement should inspire you to dream; your mission statement should inspire you to action. Your personal mission statement needs to be concise, result oriented, and unlike organizational mission statements, yours should be very personable and non-generic.

My vision statement is "From Cradles to Careers." My mission statement must be a personal call to action, remind me of my daily quest and must be personal. In addition, it must state my what (what I want to do) and my why (why I want to do it.) Therefore, it must be an "I" statement. "I" must be in the mission because it is "I" that is taking the steps on this path. Make it personal.

This is my mission for my life-changing cookie: I will seek, find, and help develop character in fatherless boys for successful careers.

My personal Vision Statement:
"From Cradles to Careers"

My personal Mission Statement:
I will seek, find and help develop fatherless boys. "

Now it's your turn, grab a pen and paper and write a personal mission statement. Get focused. Know where you want to go, make sure it has movement and it challenges you daily.

Awesome! You have a vision and mission statement, now you must do something that will remind you what it is every day. Repetition, repetition, and more repetition create good habits. The more you are reminded of your personal vision and mission statement, the more you are reminded how much you actually want it. You must have daily affirmations. I want you to wake up and go to sleep reminded of your mission, i.e., your cookie. I need you to change every password, sign in, screen saver, voice message, and social media page to reflect your vision. Every time you sign on, access your account, or just scroll the Internet you will be reminded of your personal vision and mission statement. Every morning when I sign in to get my emails or check my bank account, I type cradle. I have a daily reminder of my cookie that is attached to my everyday activities.

Let's go a step further. Since your statement can fit on a T-shirt, how about getting a T-shirt made with the vision or mission statement on it. Let that T-shirt be your inspiration to get those cookies. I want you to sleep in it, work out in it, meditate in it, and dream in it. Every time you feel like quitting or get discouraged, wear that T-shirt. By the time you get those cookies, you will need a new T-shirt because that one will be worn to shreds.

OBJECTIVES (How much of what will be accomplished by when)

Now it's about to get real. This separates the big boys and big girls from everybody else. The second step on your path to get those cookies is to define your objectives. Objectives are the things that make your vision and mission take life. Objectives are measurable results. Objectives are the things that can be expected to help you reach your desired end. Your personal objectives will detail specifics of *how much of what* will be accomplished by *when*. Once you place a timeframe on your dreams, they become goals. Without a hard deadline, you will forever be a dreamer.

48

You need concentrated and concise objectives that can be measured and celebrated when they happen. When you achieve an objective, create a method of celebration. Take yourself out to dinner, have a weekend getaway, or do like I do and create a victory dance. Get in the mirror and bust a move that symbolizes you are one step closer to getting those cookies. Make sure at the very least you have a minimum of three objectives. Keep this in the forefront of your mind — small wins lead to big victories, which builds confidence.

Here are my personal objectives for my life-changing cookie:

My personal Vision Statement:
"From Cradles to Careers"

My personal Mission Statement:
I will seek, find and help develop fatherless boys."

My personal Objectives:
- *By the end of the summer, I will identify five fatherless boys in 1st grade that I will mentor.*
- *By October, I will have a safe place to have group discussions.*

- *By December, I will have visited their school twice and taken them on two outings.*

It is totally okay if your objectives only cover a certain period of time (i.e. a year). You do not have to do everything at once. Remember what I said in Chapter 6 we are looking to win. As a matter of fact, after you have accomplished those objectives, you immediately create more that will progress you down the path to those cookies.

Just look at the progress you have made since applying yourself to be vision driven. Simply applying hard time lines will give you the much needed push to do something every day. Every day I waste or don't accomplish what I sought out to do, a young boy becomes that much closer to being a statistic. As you walk this path and your capacity expands you will no longer need outside affirmation. Your encouragement will come from shortening the distance between you and your cookies.

Your objectives have created a much-needed reason to celebrate your win. According to my personal objectives, there will be a celebration at the end of the summer, in October and another celebration in December. When I have small wins, and my objectives are satisfied, I do a victory dance. Nobody has to be watching; I just bust my 'I just won' move. I put on my vision T-shirt, pump my fist in the air and shout I am getting closer. I can see you now, in your vision T-shirt, busting your victory move and shouting I am getting closer.

STRATEGIES (*The How*)

The third step is to deal with the big question, how are you going to do what is needed to achieve your objectives. This is where many people fall short, they have a strong *What* (this is what I want to do), they have a strong *Why* (this is why I want to do it), but they have a very weak *How* (how am I going to do it).

How you plan to achieve your objectives is called a strategy. A strategy is a plan of action aimed at achieving a goal. You must have strategies. After all, this is the process of strategic planning. Pay special attention to the fact that I said *strategies* which is plural. It will take more than one. This will not be a one step process but a calculated well thought out plan that will yield positive results. You need to place heavy emphasis on defining your strategies. It will take a multitude of strategies to get you to your cookies. However, it's okay to have a few strategies for the same objective. The key is not reducing how many things you do but increasing the likelihood that your objectives are met. The strategies must detail how you will get things done. You must have a how, or you will waste valuable time. Just like your objectives detail by when, your strategies detail by how.

Strategies should give overall direction, advance the mission, minimize resistance, and fit resources and opportunities. These are crucial components to consider when you create your strategies. Absolutely everything you do should point you in the direction of getting those cookies. There is no other acceptable destination for you. Collectively, all the strategies should come together to move the mission forward.

If my mission is "to seek, find, and develop fatherless boys" and one of my objectives is to identify five fatherless boys in 1st grade that I will mentor, then one of the strategies must be *"go to a place where there are fatherless boys."* Where are these fatherless boys? Fatherless boys can be found at schools, churches or in after-school programs. I can't just walk into a school, a church or an agency and say give me five fatherless boys. I must build relationships and trust with those that oversee those intuitions. This leads me to another strategy for that objective, *"I must build relationships with institutions that have fatherless 1st grade boys."* The next question is, what will I say to those persons or what will I give them to explain my intentions? Another strategy for the same objective, *"I must create my introduction speech and pamphlets for the purpose of recruiting."* Notice how I created three strategies for the same objective? I walked myself through the process of what it would take to achieve the objective of identifying five fatherless boys in 1st grade that I will mentor.

Pay special attention to the continuity of thought from vision to mission, to objectives, and to strategies.

My personal Vision Statement:
"From Cradles to Careers"

My personal Mission Statement:
I will seek, find, and help develop fatherless boys.

My personal Objectives:
- *By the end of the summer, I will identify five fatherless boys in 1st grade that I will mentor.*

My personal strategies:
- *I must create an introduction speech and informational pamphlets for the purpose of recruiting.*
- *I must visit places where there are fatherless 1st grade boys.*
- *I must build relationships with institutions that have fatherless 1st grade boys.*

Be prepared, there will be some resistance. In Chapter 5, I discussed obstacles, challenges, and excuses you will encounter when you begin to strategize. Your strategies must align themselves with resources (people, money, power, materials, etc.). Make sure you look within yourself and evaluate your own capacities, capabilities and competencies first. You want to optimize everything you have within you before going to anyone else. People are prone to assist when they see you are giving 100 percent.

GET THOSE COOKIES

Nobody and I mean nobody will invest more into you getting your cookies than you. If that were the case, you would be munching on your cookies at this moment. If the strategy does not meet your desired mission, why are you doing it? Your strategies are where you will shift from intangible to tangible, from mental to physical, from dream to reality.

Strategies should always be determined before taking action. Never try to figure out how to do something after you have done it. I'm excited for you; you have all the necessary tools (vision, mission, objectives and strategies) to take action and get those cookies.

CHAPTER 8
The Reach Is Worth The Reward

"Sometimes the questions are complicated and the answers are simple."
~ Dr. Seuss

One of the most common mistakes that we all make is not pausing to evaluate where we are before we make our next move. Determining your current position is crucial to you staying on the path to success. At this point, any deviation from the path may set you back years or even destroy your ability to get those cookies.

I recall when I was an excited high school graduate. The atmosphere amongst my fellow graduates was electric; we had all chosen a path to what we believed would be a successful life and career. I received an academic scholarship to Alcorn State University in the beautiful state of Mississippi where I would major in Business Administration. I arrived on campus with both ambition and fear. I wanted to be a great student and also enjoy the joys of living independently for the first time in my life. Like most freshmen, I struggled with adjusting to college; trying to balance academics, along with independence and popularity was a major juggling act. I can admit that I made some bad choices that put me in a position that jeopardized my college career. I was trying to be popular and cool, and it cost me my scholarship. There are many days that I still reflect on what would have been if I had stayed at Alcorn State University and completed my education in Mississippi.

I was definitely in the right place, a university that could nurture my development, challenge me academically and socially center me. The problem was not the place; it was that I was not in the right space.

PLACE AND SPACE
ARE TWO VERY DIFFERENT THINGS.
Please take the time and read carefully to understand the difference. This is crucial for your next step to get those cookies.

Most people define place and space as the same, but you will learn they are not at all the same. And for that reason alone, we are going to take a moment to pause to gauge where you are in this process.

By definition, a place is a particular position or point.

At this point in your journey to get your cookies, you should have:

- An understanding of capacity, capability and competency (Introduction)
- A desire to get the cookies you see every day (Chapter 1)
- Identified your cookie (Chapter 2)
- Grasped how experiences and exposure have affected your passion (Chapter 3)
- Figured out how to adjust to "No's" (Chapter 4)
- Got rid of or overcome obstacles, challenges and excuses (Chapter 5)
- Determined that you're going to be a winner (Chapter 6)
- Created your own personal path to your cookie (Chapter 7)

The previous chapters were to ensure that you were in the best position to get your cookie. And at this point in the book, you should be at that place. What place is that? It is the place right beneath the cookie jar. That is the place I want you to be; in striking distance to get what you see every day but can't seem to grasp. The path you created for yourself has gotten you in the right place and proximity. You are in the very same place as I was, standing in my Auntie's kitchen looking up at those beautiful, moist chocolate chip cookies. The difference between you and I is that you have tools that will shorten the distance between you and the cookies.

Space is defined as the freedom and scope to live, think, and develop in a way that suits one's ability to become.

It makes no sense to be in the right place and not take the necessary direct actions to propel you forward. If my cookie is to be a life-changing mentor, a direct action would be actually to go to schools to find fatherless boys. This action is necessary to push me towards achieving a particular objective. If the action does not get you closer to the cookies, then it is a total waste of time.

There is a spiritual component that lies within each of us. Regardless of what you call it or identify it as, it has the unique responsibility to inspire and motivate. It gives confidence, direction, the courage to reach, and radiates faith. It is an inner strength that gives a sense of self, that pushes you to take direct actions and make things happen in your life. This spiritual component gives you the ability to go within yourself so that you will be able to extend beyond where you currently are and reach. You are in the right place physically, you are in the right place mentally, now you need to get in the right space. This is all designed to shorten the distance and help you get your cookies.

The right spiritual space will give you the courage to take direct action to get that cookie. It will be a continuous area or expanse that is free, available, or unoccupied by negative thoughts, negative energy, and non-productive people. The last thing you want to do is get to this place and allow outside influences to deter you from taking direct actions. Find you a place of solitude, comfort, and support that will consistently stimulate you into direct action. This is imperative for the next phase in your path to success.

Now, you are in the right place, and you have created a healthy and positive space for you to get those cookies. You must now consider which of the direct actions are best to shorten the distance between where you are and your cookie. My challenge as I stood looking up at my Auntie's cookies was not just the fact that she said "No" but also my inability to reach the cookies. If I could have just gotten to the jar, I would have gotten those wonderful cookies.

The name of the game is get to the jar! And, shortening the distance between you and the jar is the best path to that goal.

There are four direct actions that you can take to shorten the distance and get you those cookies. These four direct actions will be the focus of the rest of our journey. You have the distinct opportunity to do all or just one direct action. But you MUST do something.

You must:
- **Grow Up**
- **Jump Up**
- **Pull Up**
- **Join Up**

This is what it takes to get to the jar and ultimately your cookie. Do not forget our direction is UP!

GET THOSE COOKIES

In these next few chapters, we will delve deep into each action that will get us on the path of shortening the distance between you and your cookies. These actions take you from talking about getting cookies to doing something about getting them. For some of you, it may take a combination of direct actions, and that's okay. Today you are in the best place and space to get your cookie.

Chapter 9
You Got To Be This Tall To Ride

"You must be standing in a hole boy.
Everything I say goes Zoom,
right over your head."
~ Foghorn J. Leghorn

I remember as a child one of the greatest thrills in life was to go to the amusement park. I would work and save all my money from doing odd jobs in the neighborhood. Each dollar I earned from delivering papers, cutting grass or running errands for the adults on my block would be designated for Six Flags Great America. All the kids in the neighborhood would be abuzz about the new and exciting rides at Six Flags. We would talk about how we were going to ride each ride at least three times. We would tease each other about being scared to ride on roller coasters and give each other the triple-dog-dare to ride. The triple-dog-dare is infamous for the sole reason that you cannot back down from it. Once issued, the triple-dog-dare has no counteraction and must be implemented and/or carried out.

After what seemed to be months of saving and preparation, we were boarding the bus to Six Flags. We would take the bus ride with great anticipation looking out the window for the massive wooden roller coaster called the American Eagle. The site of the American Eagle was our marker that we had arrived. The bus pulled to the main entrance, and we rushed off the bus straight to the ticket booth to purchase our tickets; my excitement was indescribable. There we were tickets in hand, triple-dog-dare on our mind and excitement in our belly racing to the first roller coaster. We made it to the roller coaster, ready to get in line with all smiles and sheer joy. The joy was temporary because as we approached the riding zone, there was a wooden caricature of Foghorn Leghorn saying, "you got to be this tall to ride this ride." WOW!!! Access denied.

Waited all summer, worked odd jobs, saved my money to buy a ticket, got my friends together, took the two-hour ride, and identified the marker. I could actually see others getting on the ride that I couldn't get on. Why? Because "you got to be this tall to ride." It made no difference that I had stood in line; I still had to be this tall to ride. I couldn't ride with anyone because on this ride I had to qualify to ride on my own. It made no difference who my parents were, who I was with, how much I paid, how long I waited or how long it took me to get there. The fact remained, "you have to be this tall to ride on this ride," no exceptions.

The first direct action we will explore is straightforward. You can see it, but you can't ride because you have to be this tall to ride. For multiple reasons, you are not the right height. Our first direct action is you got to GROW UP. You can get what you see and what seems out of reach by simply growing up.

Now how simple is that? Just grow up, and you will be able to reach those things that you see and desire. That's so simple that I could stop right here, but if I did it would leave multiple unanswered questions like:

- What does it mean to grow up?
- Why am I too short?
- Do I need to grow in stature, wisdom, character or faith?
- How do I start to grow?
- When do I know that I have grown enough?
- And the mother of all questions, how long will it take me to grow?

The answer to all of the above questions rests in one scenario. You continue to grow based on how you deal with pain, difficulties and hard times. Your growth starts when you can process through, learn more and become better in the midst of pain, difficulties and hard times. Pain is a great motivator, difficulty is a great educator, and hard times are a great stimulator. When pain, difficulties and hard times enter your life, they will either stunt your growth or force you to take the necessary steps to grow. The primary reason you are vertically challenged is because pain, difficulties and hard times are controlling and shaping your perception; which subsequently affects your decision-making and ultimately your direct actions.

You start to grow when you come face to face with your pain, confront your difficulties and accost your hard times. Growth comes in owning the feelings associated with embracing and learning from your pain, difficulties and hard times. Say it! It's mine. This is my pain. These are my difficulties. These are my hard times. Collectively the pain, difficulties and hard times I encountered were designed to stimulate my growth. I accepted them, I embraced them, I owned them, and most importantly, I learned to appreciate them.

For the majority of my childhood and my early adult life I believed my growth was stunted by the absence of my father. My parents divorced when I was four years old, and it affected me deeply. My attitude, behavior, and perception were directly connected to me questioning, why did he leave me and why was I not good enough. I distinctively remember praying with my mother and asking God to please allow me to see my father before he dies.

To be totally honest, I blamed him for all the bad decisions, bad turns and inadequacies in my life. I constantly thought to myself, if I only had a Dad things would be different, and I would be better. The motive of my prayers was not solely to see my father, but I wanted to curse him to his face. I wanted to let him have it to the tenth power. I wanted him to know how his little boy felt about him leaving and never coming back. I wanted to curse him for all the birthdays, graduations, baseball games and award ceremonies he missed. Yes, the real reason I prayed to God was to get an opportunity to curse my father.

Well, God answered my prayer, and I got the chance to see my father before he died. We received a call that he was dying, and he wanted to see his children before he passed. I imagine that just as I was affected by pain, difficulties and hard times so too was my father. I believe our lack of relationship truly pained him and stunted his growth as well. So here you have two vertically challenged people coming together after twenty years of pain. I will never forget approaching his building and climbing the long flight of stairs: twenty-three stairs to be exact. I counted each step because those steps represented my ascension to freedom and the release of my anger associated with the absence of my father. Finally, after twenty years I had come face to face with my father. As you can imagine, the emotion was overwhelming and the moment was surreal.

Everything in my life up to that point was to prove to him that I was worth him staying around. I was auditioning for a part that did not exist. I was trying out for a team that I would never play on. I was seeking attention from someone that was not paying attention. It was time for me to grow up. I needed to get taller than this situation. I had to live, think and have faith above where I currently existed. I had to dig into the sacred spiritual space within and make a decision to grow. I owned my true feelings. I had to admit that I didn't want to curse him out, but what I wanted was a gigantic hug. I needed a 20-year hug to soothe all the pain, difficulties and hard times that I had experienced. When he gave me that hug, I forgave him, and I started to grow.

My entire life from the time I was four years old until I was twenty-four, I blamed him. I had embraced the notion that I was living my life for someone else. It was hard for me to let go of the blame because to release the blame would mean that I would have to grow up and be responsible for my actions. I had been coming up short in many areas in my life and as it turned out it was not his fault after all; it was my decisions. It was my internalization of the pain, difficulties and hard times. Obtaining my cookies was not the responsibility of my father; these were my cookies. My dreams and aspirations belonged to me, and my father's negligence had no influence or authority over me any longer. If I was going to enjoy the rollercoaster called life, I had to be reminded that I had to be "this tall to ride on this ride." My acceptance and acknowledgment allowed me to begin to grow in capacity, competency, and capability.

GET THOSE COOKIES

I challenge you to grow in the areas that you are weak. I challenge you to grow in the places that have brought you the most pain. Acknowledge its presence deep within the spaces that leave us the most vulnerable and insecure. If you grow through the pain, press your way through difficulties and learn from hard times you will get a little closer to that cookie jar. And the closer you get to the cookie jar the closer you get to the cookies.

CHAPTER 10
I Believe I Can Fly

*"You wanna fly, you got to give up the
shit that weighs you down."*
~ Toni Morrison

As you may have already discovered, I have very vivid images of my childhood. As a matter of fact, most of us have taken our childhood memories and images and transferred those into adult lessons, behaviors and beliefs. It has been proven that our core beliefs stem from childhood experiences. It is those core beliefs that must be challenged and changed in our quest for those cookies.

Let me share one of those images and lessons with you. In the backyard of the home I grew up in, we had an assortment of fruit trees: peach, cherry, apple and pear. I could look out any window in the summer and see fruit. Naturally, when I ventured into the yard, we would have a lawn full of fruit that had fallen.

My mother always emphatically told me to never eat the fruit that fell to the ground. No matter how good it appeared it was not to be eaten. Only eat the fruit that was picked from the tree, and the best fruit was at the top. The fruit that was out of reach, the fruit that you had to put in the most effort to get, was the sweetest. At the same time my mother would say, "Boy, don't let me catch you climbing those trees." I was in a conflicting situation, on one hand the best fruit was at the top of the tree, out of my reach and on the other hand, I could not climb the tree to get to it. At that moment I wished I could fly. If I could fly, I could get to the top, get what was best and come back down and enjoy it. Reality sunk in. I couldn't fly to the top, I couldn't climb to the top, and I couldn't eat from the ground. How would I ever get some good fruit? I had to learn how to jump.

If I could just jump high enough, I could get a piece of the good sweet fruit. This is the exact same position you are in today. You can't fly so you need to jump. You need to take a leap of faith. With so many things we desire above our heads, jumping may be the best solution.

Jumping is not something we do naturally. Jumping is an acquired skill. I needed to learn how to jump to get the things that were above my head. You'd think you wouldn't really need to be taught how to jump; surely it's a natural thing, isn't it? Well like most things, it both is and isn't. Yes, we automatically move to jumping when we explore movement as toddlers. My toddler son jumps all over the place. He jumps up on the counter; he jumps on the bed, and most of all he jumps on me. If you were to spend a few hours with him, you might conclude that he is a great jumper. But because he jumps doesn't mean he jumps efficiently. And the same holds true for adults. We don't know how to jump utilizing our capacities, capabilities, and competencies. We are just jumping with no aim and no strategy. In fact, it's a rare individual that can jump strongly and with precision without any instruction. If that's you, that's great! But the rest of us would benefit from learning the fundamentals of skillful and powerful jumping techniques.

There are three things that are essential to a great jump. The first thing we need to establish is the foundation. You need a solid base to push off that will propel you up towards your cookie. The foundation we have set in our previous chapters is rock solid.

Your foundation is a mixture of:
- A well thought out Personal Path
- An awesome Vision and Mission Statement
- Measurable objectives
- Comprehensive strategies
- Courage and confidence in self
- Revived passion and purpose

o   Being in the right place and space

Your foundation will support your jumping efforts.

The second thing that you need to make a skillful and powerful jump is momentum. Momentum consists of energy, force, strength, and velocity.

I know you have the energy and the enthusiasm to jump up and get your cookie. You should have a renewed energy every time you put on your T-shirt and do your victory dance. You have the energy to jump!

I know the force is with you. Winners force issues to create opportunities and to get the edge over their opponents. You have this power to force some things to happen for you. This is not the moment to be timid or polite. You may never be at this juncture again in your life. You have the force to jump!

I know you feel the strength that has come from your hard work. The strength you have gotten from facing your pain, difficulties, and hard times. The strength you get from that voice within you encouraging you each and every day to get your cookie. The strength of knowing what you want and knowing how close you are to getting your cookie. The strength of overcoming obstacles, challenges and excuses. You are strong! By this point in the journey, all the weak people have quit. Your strength has gotten you to striking distance of that cookie jar. You have the strength to jump!

Do you know the definition of velocity? Velocity is the speed of something in a given direction. Let's insert you into the definition. Velocity is the speed in which you are moving towards your cookie. You need to determine what is your base operating speed. Only you can determine how fast you need to be going. I strongly suggest that you go faster than you normally operate. Challenge yourself to pick up speed and increase your velocity. You cannot create velocity by standing still. You have to be moving at an accelerated pace. Do not move so slow that you miss the chance to jump. You have the velocity and speed to jump.

Take advantage of the momentum that has been generated. It is time for you to take the jump of your life!

You have a strong foundation, and you have the momentum to make a powerful jump. What you need next is the proper technique to aim your jump. The third element of a skillful and powerful jump is aim. You have a specific mission; you have pre-calculated objectives, and you have well thought out strategies to get that cookie. You are not jumping just to jump. You do not have the time or energy to keep jumping and missing. You need to jump with accuracy and precision so that you do not lose momentum.

Are you jumping up to something that is stationary or moving? If you are aiming towards a moving target timing is of the essence. For example, my "Cradles to Careers" life-changing cookie in which I mentor fatherless boys, I will need funding. I will need financial resources for things like field trips, college tours, materials, and transportation. The funding resources all have timelines on when to apply for funds to assist my mission. Those funds are a moving target. There is a precise time that I must jump to get those monies. If I don't get the funds now, I may very well have to wait an extended period of time before they become available again. My aim is crucial because if I don't have everything else in order (i.e. applications, references, business plans, program narrative, etc.), my jump would be in vain. Know what you are aiming for before you jump.

GET THOSE COOKIES

I can see you looking up at those cookies just as I looked up at that fruit. Calculating and convincing yourself that you can jump up and get that cookie. You can do it! All of those small wins are about to lead to a great victory. Cookie in hand, lock in, focus, concentrate, and remember what it took for you to get to this moment, then jump like you have never jumped before.

CHAPTER 11
Broken Crayons Still Color

"We are all a little broken,
But the last time I checked
broken crayons still color."
~ Trent Shelton

I have shared a few of my life experiences for the sole purpose of reflecting on what I would consider defining moments in my life. A defining moment is a point at which the essential nature or character of a person is revealed or identified. These moments change the perspective and the course of a person's life. It is these defining moments that cause one to stop completely , evaluate, assess and think about the direction of their life and how that is tied to their purpose. In your defining moments are the questions of capacity, capability, competency, vision, mission, objectives, strategies, space and place. The defining moment in one's life is a powerful tool to keep or redirect you to your path of success. Defining moments are so full of truths, honesty, and clarity that they cannot be denied, but they can be ignored. As a warning to you, please do not continue to ignore these moments because they can mean death to your purpose, your dreams, your relationships and quite frankly your life.

When I was twenty-six, I had such a defining moment, my "basement experience." One of the darkest days of my life was on March 17, 1995. I was sitting in a friend's basement, on a milk crate, next to a puddle of water, dressed in business suit, shirt, tie, and polished shoes and I was bragging. I was bragging about how fortunate, smart, and educated I was. I was informing my audience of friends that they needed to do something with their lives. They should be like me have a job, a car, a family, and make something of themselves. I was giving this motivational speech all while I was holding a plate of cocaine in one hand, a marijuana joint in the other and cup of whiskey resting at my feet. I had been getting high on cocaine and drinking liquor for two straight days. My beeper was full of pages from my beloved wife, who I knew had contacted my mother and my siblings to inform them I was nowhere to be found. I had completely isolated myself into this basement, and as I sat in a drug induced stupor, I was lecturing on the qualities of life.

Right in the midst of my disquisition, one of my fellow audience members (aka a fellow drunk), as he passed me a bottle said with such disdain, "If you got

all of that shit, why the hell you down here with us?"
Boom! A bomb on my faux reality had been dropped.
The anger was immediate. How dare this low life, this
drunk, this person that should just appreciate my mere
presence and the sincerity of my words question me?
What the hell does he mean, why am I in this
basement, sitting on a milk crate, in a business suit,
shirt, tie and polished shoes, sniffing cocaine, smoking
joints and drinking liquor? I cannot believe he had the
audacity to ask me that question as my pager rings, my
wife worries, and my mother prays for my safety. I was
livid, I was appalled, but I was faced with some real
truths. The truth was that question brought everything
I was trying to run from into that basement. I know my
dear mother was in anguish praying for her son. I know
my wife who had so many times tried to encourage me
and tell me that I was slowly destroying myself; would
not give up and was still out hunting for me to save
me. I knew my son was waiting with faith that his
father would come back and give him that blue juice
and a bag of chips. The hardest truth was, I was not
better than anyone in that basement.

After the anger, and after the truth, came the hard
questions. First, why am I down here in this basement
sitting on a milk crate like it's a throne, in a now very
wrinkled and soiled business suit, an unbuttoned dirty
shirt, and only God knows where I put that tie.
Polished shoes thrown in the corner, sniffing cocaine,
smoking joints and drinking liquor when I have so much

potential? My life has been reduced to an illusion, and he just showed me a mirror, and I hate the reflection.

Second, do I really need some help? I've been drugging and drinking since I was twelve. I wasn't getting high; I was actually getting very low. That's fourteen years of trying to escape, mask my feelings and live well below my expectation.

And the most important question of them all, where is the blue juice and the bag of chips my six-year-old son had asked me to bring him when I left two days ago?

I didn't have the blue juice or the bag of chips. I didn't even have a dollar to buy them. I had a grandiose attitude, lectures, the corporate look, the college degree, but I didn't even have one dollar to get my son a blue juice and a bag of chips. I had spent all my money on drugs and alcohol. While I was making "milk crate" speeches, my six-year-old son was waiting on what I promised. There is a high cost for low living and I was paying the price. I had hit rock bottom, and it was at this bottom that my life would be defined. I was faced with these truths, either go on to the bitter end of jails, intuitions, death or find a new way to live. I needed a pull up.

All of us get to a certain place in life where we need to pull ourselves up. We are living in holes beneath our capacities, capabilities, and competencies. These holes have no space for visions, dreams, family and success. I know you can see the light peering down on you, I know you can hear the voices of loved ones cheering for you and I know you feel that inner strength within you. It's time for a pull up.

Whether you have been knocked down, slipped down or just laid down, you can get up. You can pull yourself out of that rut. You can rise above that self-inflicted pain, those moments of regrets and those times of defeat.

I made myself a promise in that defining moment surrounded by truths and hard to answer questions; I would never break a promise to my children again. I have never broken that vow. It's been twenty-one years and I have never ventured in that basement again. It's been twenty-one years since I have done any drugs or alcohol. And in those twenty-one years my son has had quite a few blue juices and bags of chips. My world and my stage have gotten larger than a basement and the seats I sit in are much more comfortable than a milk crate.

In order to pull yourself up, you must make a promise that will kill you to break. Put some distance between you and your basement experience. Everyone's pull up is different, I went to 12 step meetings, I prayed, I went back to school, I spent more time with my family, I connected with a crowd that had high expectations, and I got busy living and stop trying to kill myself. I pulled myself out of that basement and became a father, a husband, a son, a motivational speaker, a graduate, a pastor, a community activist and the list continues. The best way to do this is one day at a time. The further you get away from the basement the closer you get to the cookie jar.

GET THOSE COOKIES

As you gaze up to that cookie jar at this precise time in your life, this is a defining moment. Yes, you have been broken, but you still have some color in you. Pull yourself up and realize that you are in the right place to go for those cookies. As you inch closer and closer to that cookie jar, don't forget your promise. Remember how it felt in the basement of your life. And as you are pulling yourself out of that hole, keep talking to yourself saying these words, "those are my cookies, and I'm going to get them."

CHAPTER 12
Line Up In "2's"

"There are two questions that we have to ask ourselves. The 1st is, "Where am I going?" and the 2nd is, "Who will go with me?" If you ever get these questions in the wrong order, you are in trouble."
~ Howard Thurman

One of my proudest moments as a child was open house at school. I must admit I was an exceptional student. Learning seemed to come naturally to me, and I grasp new ideas and concepts relatively easy. I was considered one of the "gifted" students in the school. A gifted student was one that scores in the upper percentile on standardized test and is consistently on the honor roll. Open house was the day that all exceptional work was placed on display so that parents could see. I was proud that quite a few of my papers and projects were prominently featured. In conjunction with open house, it was typically the day that parents picked up report cards and had parent/teacher conferences.

My mother would be beaming with pride and joy at her son's work and all the "A's" I had received that marking period. It was an awesome day until it came time to have the parent/teacher conference. This was the moment that my mother and teacher would discuss the other side of the report card.

The other side of the report card had a section that evaluated conduct, behavior, and social traits. This section did not have letter grades but was marked with a check to indicate a need for improvement or a plus to indicate commendable development.

This section had topics such as:
- o Follows directions
- o Works diligently
- o Shows consideration for others
- o Assumes responsibilities
- o Respects private and public property
- o Works and plays well with others

I would receive plus marks on all of them except, you guessed it, works and plays well with others. For some reason, I just never fit into crowds and had a difficult time teaming with others. I was just under the belief that I could just do it better by myself. I believe many of us had a similar thought process and that is why the idea of teams were constantly reinforced throughout our formative years.

It started with works and plays well with others, and then transitioned to get a partner and line up, recess partners, science fair partners, locker partners, small group research papers, and roommates. Consistently, I was encouraged to connect and team up to work and play well with others.

On the contrary, as we were being indoctrinated with the concept of team, we were equally persuaded to be an individual. I still hear words like: make your own decisions, don't follow the crowd and the big one, "If all your friends jump off a bridge would you do that too?" These were conflicting portrayals; on the one hand, be a team player and on the other hand be an individual. I became confused as to when I was supposed to be a team player and when I was supposed to be an individual. When was I supposed to go along with the team or when I was supposed to take the lead? These grammar school check marks and plus marks turned into adult work place evaluations, which were directly connected to my job performance, promotions and ultimately my income. Am I a team player?

When we think of a team, most of us have images of a group of people all equally working to achieve a shared desired outcome. Everyone on the team equally contributes his or her talents and expertise so that the team is successful or victorious. That's the team we imagined. In actuality, the team concept is building support around one exceptional individual. This one exceptional individual primarily has the bulk of the talent but needs additional people to lend their capacities, capabilities, and competencies to their talents, to be successful or victorious. This clearly dilutes the imagery of a team containing persons of equal contributions. The team concept that is prevalent today caters to the exceptional individual and what small support is needed for that person to make the entire group successful. The idea of a team is only beneficial to them because they can't do it by themselves. They are not necessarily a team player, but they understand that a team is a must for them to achieve success.

I am introducing you to a new concept that will replace the "team up" notion. It will allow you to remain an exceptional individual, save some time and get assistance. How about we call it "Join Up." To join something indicates that it is already in motion and it is progressing toward a specific goal. The vision, mission, objectives, and strategies are all in place and what is needed is someone to "join up" and give it that extra boost to eliminate the distance between where you are currently and the cookie jar. Just imagine two exceptional individuals joining together because you both want the same cookie. You both believe in the same vision, have the same mission; agree on the same objectives and strategies. You'll have a clear understanding of each other's capabilities, capacities, and competencies. And even more important, both of you are in the same place and space right beneath the cookie jar. Let me remind you this is not about competition; this is about completion. Let's join up.

There is one major consideration that must be taken before "joining up" with another exceptional individual: that consideration is trust. This is major and cannot be minimized. Do you completely trust each other? After all, this is the very moment you both have been dreaming about, and you did not come this far to be defrauded or misled. You are trusting them, and they are trusting you with all their hard work, pain, tears, victories, and hope. And that trust will immediately be tested because a crucial decision must be made immediately. There are only two positions a person can take when they join up with another. Either you are the person that is helping to boost the person up, or you are the person being boosted. Both positions require a tremendous amount of trust in the other person.

The person being boosted must trust that the person that is boosting them has the strength to hold them up for a sustained period of time and not drop them. The last thing you want to do is to be dropped this close to the cookie jar. Can I trust you when we join up that you can hold me up? Also, the person that is doing the boosting must have complete trust that when the person that he or she is boosting gets to the cookie jar, they will get a cookie for the both of them. Let's be honest we didn't come this far to share a cookie. I want my own cookie. Can I trust that when you make it to the cookie jar that you will get enough for us both? This is both the strength and the challenge of joining up. And the decision that must be made is who will be in each position.

GET THOSE COOKIES

Let's face it, sometimes after we have grown up, jumped up or even pulled ourselves up we still fall short of the cookie jar. I completely understand your desire to want to get the cookie all by yourself. I get it. We don't work or play well with others.

But at this precise moment in your life, you should determine whether or not you can do it by yourself, and if not, join up with somebody. That's being smart. As I consistently stated throughout this book, the name of the game is shortening the distance between you and the cookie jar. If that distance can be shortened or possibly eliminated by joining with a like-minded individual, by all means, do it. Do not hesitate, get those cookies.

THE FINAL CHAPTER
Get Ready, Get Set, Go...

*"Never go back for less, just because you're
too impatient to wait for best"*
~ Unknown

satisfaction |satis'fakSHən|
The fulfillment of one's wishes, expectations, or
needs, or the pleasure derived from something

One of the things I learned early in my life is the power of words. Words have the unique ability to shape, mold, build and construct; but on the opposite end they can destroy, distort and tear down. A single word by itself carries the authority to have this effect on a person's life. Single words like love, hate, beautiful, ugly, courageous, and fear all have these qualities. One word can change the determination and mindset of an individual. Now, just imagine how impactful a string of words, a sentence if you will, has on a person's psyche. If an entire sentence is spoken into a person's life, it could have long-lasting, life-changing ramifications. This is why we are consistently cautioned to be careful what we say to a person. Because the age-old adage "Sticks and stones may break my bones but words will never hurt me." Words do hurt, especially when they come from people we value.

Words and sentences from people we care about carry a great amount of weight in our decisions and choices. Their input and opinions matter to us. Their words motivate and inspire us. Because we know what they say to us is in complete love and truth. Children have this magnificent power to lift us and motivate us continuously. Children do not have filters, they see, and they say. This is what makes them so wonderful.

I remember when I started my second business, Brothers Helping Brothers Transportation. My first business was a complete flop, Dukes Mortgage Financing. In my preparation to launch my second business, I did all the usual requisites: business research, marketing strategy, and financial planning. I was determined to be successful. In the midst of all my due diligence, my three kids were constantly running around doing what kids do, making a lot of noise and disturbing everything in sight. At the midpoint of their mass destruction of the house, they turned their attention towards me. All three marched upon and asked "Daddy what are you doing." And I responded I am starting a new business and we are going to be rich. They immediately started jumping around and shouting we are going be rich. My youngest child, Emerald looked at me with the biggest smile and said, "Daddy I want to help." I looked at my three children and said, "Each of you will have a key position in the business." Austin, you are the oldest so you will be the Vice President, Morgon, you will be the Chairman of the Board of Directors and Emerald you will be the Treasurer.

For the next two weeks they ran around the house shouting we are going to be rich, we got a business, I am the vice president, I am the chairman, and I am the treasurer. It brought pure delight to me that they were so excited about the business. But as time wore down and all the things that were supposed to be simple became hard, I became discouraged and frustrated. Each day brought a new struggle and a new challenge; it seemed as though this business would never start.

One of the last items I needed was to obtain a business license. For me to get a business license I needed to be incorporated. I had to incorporate Brothers Helping Brothers Transportation. Therefore, I had to drive three hundred miles to the state capitol in Springfield, Illinois to become a legitimate business. I grabbed my vice president, my chairman of the board and my treasurer and piled into the minivan and headed south. My faith, confidence, and esteem were at an all-time low. If this did not work, I was quitting. I was ready and willing to accept that I sucked as an entrepreneur. After this little road trip, I was going to polish up my resume and go back to corporate America.

Then all of a sudden something miraculous happened. I started listening to the words of my children. I shut down the voices in my head and focused on what they were saying. They were in constant chatter about how rich they were going to be and what they were going to buy with all the money. They asked me a million questions about the business, their functions, and their rewards. They argued amongst themselves about who had the most important job. Their words encouraged me, lifted me and revived me. Out of the mouth of babes, I regained my focus and my determination.

I needed my kids to remind me of my dream. They had the audacity to believe what I had told them. When we piled in that minivan, doubt, frustration and lack of will all climbed in with us. But the more they talked, the better I felt.

I arrived in Springfield pumped up with three enthusiastic children by my side. As, I completed the incorporation paperwork, the woman behind the desk stated to me, "Sir, you could have done this paperwork in Chicago." What she didn't know is I needed the ride. My kid's expectations and my dream needed to take a long ride together.

On my way home, driving north on Interstate 55, after I had given them happy meals and they had fallen sound to sleep in the backseat, I looked in my rearview mirror and saw their hope. I looked at all the road in front of me and embraced all my potential. I had a smile that was met with a tear.

I didn't have any customers, I didn't have any vans, I didn't have any money, and I didn't have any employees; but I had their belief and my hope. It was the same feeling I had after I had strolled across my auntie's yard, climbed into the back seat of my mother's car and rubbed my pocket. I had a cookie. I was satisfied.

THE AUTHOR

Dr. J. Edward Dukes began his pilgrimage of faith early in life. This faith walk has taken him through many trials, tribulations, celebrations and victories. As a senior pastor, mentor, advocate for social justice and motivational speaker he has become an expert in "passion" development.

On March 18, 1995, Dr. Dukes surrendered to the mandate on his life and began a journey of recovery and restoration. He has become a world-renowned motivational speaker and life coach in the fields of substance abuse and self-help. These speaking engagements have taken him to over 100 cities, 36 states and 9 countries. He has spoken to audiences that range from 1 to well over 10,000.

This unique gift has allowed many to hear the gut-wrenching truth about the horrors of addiction. With well over 200 messages in circulation around the world, these messages have liberated thousands, restored many families and united countless others with their passion.

Dr. Dukes' unique style of communication and counseling keeps him in high demand at educational, self-help, religious and leadership conferences. Dr. Dukes continues to inspire many through his social media weekly blog, "The Butt Naked Truth."

Dr. Dukes' primary mission in life is to assure that every person is connected to his or her life's passion. Whether your passion needs to be identified, is dormant, or needs direction, he wants to help navigate you to that end.

His educational background includes a doctor of divinity from United Theological Seminary, a master of theological study from McCormick Theological Seminary, a master of arts in counseling from Chicago State University and a bachelor of science in business administration from Chicago State University. Dr. Dukes and his wife, Christy, live in Chicago, Illinois, with their five children. You can learn more about Dr. Dukes' great work by visiting www.drjeddukes.com.

REFERENCE

Flexner, Stuart Berg. "New Oxford American Dictionary" Oxford University Press. 2001

Online Resources:

How Stuff Works. Ronca, Debra. 10 Acquired Tastes
http://recipes.howstuffworks.com/10-acquired-tastes.htm

The Community Tool Box is a service of the Work Group for Community Health and Development at the University of Kansas.   Kansas Health Foundation. *VMOSA: An approach to strategic planning.* Wichita, KS: Kansas Health Foundation.
http://ctb.ku.edu/en/table-of-contents/structure/strategic-planning/vmosa/main

The Services of
Dr. J. Edward Dukes Consulting

*"I Love You And There Is Nothing
You Can Do About That"*

Dr. Dukes has only one product — **PASSION**. However, he delivers this product through three distinctive approaches:

1. *Consultations (Individual & Group):* Every consultation is centered on the three key components to identify passion, which are Capacity, Capability, and Competency. This will formulate a success plan for self-help and personal development.

2. *Speaking Engagements (Keynote Speaker):* Dr. Dukes' demanding conference speaking schedule covers a broad-spectrum of audiences i.e., corporations, nonprofits, athletics, churches, self-help and other organizations.

3. *Workshops, Webinars and Training Events:* These dynamic settings allow Dr. Dukes to give a more intensive and comprehensive dialogue on his works through group interaction and hands on applications.

To invite Dr. Dukes To Be With You
Email: drjedwarddukes@gmail.com or
Visit: drjedwarddukes.com

The Butt Naked Truth
with Dr J.Edward Dukes

The Only Place You Are Guaranteed To Hear The Truth

Each week Dr. J. Edward Dukes presents his video blog to enlighten many on the topics of relationships, politics, religion, community and many more subjects.

Join the conversation that has captured the intention and imagination of social media

Every Tuesday you can hear "The Butt Naked Truth with Dr. J. Edward Dukes"

The Butt Naked Truth

Dr. J Edward Dukes Channel

@DrJEDukes

CPSIA information can be obtained
at www.ICGtesting.com
Printed in the USA
FFOW05n1126211216